THE END OF ANXIETY
ANXIETY
Calming Your Anxious Mind

ISBN-13: 978-0-9994972-1-0

THE END OF ANXIETY

Calming Your Anxious Mind

Manaka Unsui
Jissen Kobudo Instructor, Head of the Jinenkan

English translation by Robert R. Gray
Jinenkan Dojo-cho, Jinenkan Menkyo Kaiden

About Manaka Unsui

Manaka Sensei, who also goes by the martial name "Unsui," founded the Jinenkan in 1996. The purpose of the organization is to allow students to study the martial arts of old Japan freely and unhindered under his guidance. Unsui has over 50 years of experience in kobudo, the traditional martial arts of Japan.

About This Translation

It has been an honor to translate this book for my martial arts instructor, Manaka Unsui. The translation of this book went smoothly due to having direct access to the author to ask questions and clarify points. However, in a couple areas I did extra research to get a deeper grasp on what he was discussing. In the places I thought the additional information would be helpful to the reader, I added a *translator's note*. The notes are located at the end of the relevant sections. They are marked with an asterisk* and written all in italics. They are not in the author's original work.

Robert R. Gray

Contents

1

Foreword

When we meet someone for the first time, participate in a competition, or compete against others, our heart pounds, our mouth dries, and our hands sweat. This response is generally referred to as *agari* in Japanese, and it is a natural, physiological response that can happen to anyone. In English, agari corresponds to anxiety or stress that rises when under pressure. In addition, no matter how many times people experience it, they may feel this anxiety whenever they are put into a new environment. Therefore, instead of trying to suppress it, it is better to either minimize it or quickly enter into a state of *heijoshin*, a term which I will explain later. I researched for several years if there was a way to enter this state instantly. If it were possible, we could have very satisfying results in our daily lives.

Top class athletes have the ability to repeat the same motion over and over again. The inability to do the movement incorrectly is due to the autonomic nervous system, which I shall describe later. This is why I believe people who can set a world record during the actual event, could also set the record during training.

Three years ago, when I was a graduate research student at the University of Tsukuba, I studied the ultimate goal of kobudo: attaining the states of *mushin*, *heijoshin*, and *fudoshin*. Through the use of comprehensive human science, we developed a way to generate the state of kakusei-mushin. In this book, I shall go one step further and explain simple methods that anyone can use. These methods include learning how to apply autogenic training, mindfulness, and kakusei-mushin. In other words, they involve learning to focus oneself. This is very important but can be difficult to achieve. I will elaborate on these methods in this book.

2

What is Anxiety?

In the previous section, I mentioned the troublesome word *agari* which referred to the stress and anxiety that is caused when one is under pressure. To put it more concretely, it is the condition of being high strung or losing one's cool. It is the condition where your face turns pale and your hands and feet shake; your heart beats fast and your palms and face sweat. I think everyone has experienced this more or less at some point in their lives. During these times, what is happening inside our bodies? Let's look at both the physiological side and the mental side.

First, I will describe what happens inside the body when we feel stress or pressure. Which **hormones** are related to stress? The first is **cortisol.** This is because the adrenal glands secrete hormones which cause anxiety and tension. They are the source of the stress hormones and increase the level of tension. The internal secretion system changes to increase cortisol, which then alters alertness and perception levels. In other words, it is called a "stress hormone" because it increases when the body is stressed. In addition, this hormone regulates metabolism of blood sugar, lipids, and proteins in the body. It also regulates blood pressure, temperature, and increases the heart rate. As a result, it has the ability to preserve life despite outside disturbances such as changes in temperature and so forth. The resulting stress appears in the form of becoming high strung, losing your cool, your face turning pale, your hands and feet shaking, your heart beating fast, your palms and face sweating, and so on.

On the other hand, it has been shown that **the secretion of cortisol is suppressed when a meditative state is reached.** Learning and memory functions in the hippocampus also improve. We will discuss this meditative state in more detail later.

The second hormone is **dopamine. Dopamine is often released when you are exposed to sunshine, immersed in your hobbies, filled with desire, achieving a goal, exercising moderately, meditating or practicing mindfulness, listening to music etc. The regulation of this hormone is related to pleasure, ambition, and learning. It is the hormone that generates motivation and also generates a state of stress and tension.** However, over-eating and over-drinking have a negative effect on dopamine.

Dopamine is one of the neurotransmitters generated in the sympathetic nervous system and is metabolized into important **noradrenaline** and **adrenaline** that activate the mind and body. Noradrenaline is a substance of the sympathetic nervous system and plays a role in activating thought and consciousness as a hormone in the brain. In particular, it is secreted frequently when you feel danger, anxiety, fear or anger. It is also secreted when concentration is needed.

Adrenaline is secreted when we do extreme exercise, are in fear for our lives, or are in a competition, etc. Noradrenaline changes to adrenaline in the adrenal medulla and circulates throughout the body, signaling preparation for battle.

As a result, blood pressure rises, the heart rate increases, and concentration improves. Furthermore, the capillaries contract to minimize bleeding and reduce any pain caused by injury.

In addition, when the **parasympathetic system** is activated, the activity of the **sympathetic system** is suppressed and the physiological phenomenon is settled. Therefore, in order to calm your feelings, it is important to activate the parasympathetic nervous system. In other words, it is important to relax your mind. For this reason, top athletes can be seen implementing ways to relax themselves, such as listening to music, just before the start of a competition.

When the sympathetic nervous system becomes active, heart rate, body temperature, and blood pressure all rise quickly. Symptoms such as palpitations and trembling appear. Conversely, if only the parasympathetic system becomes activated, the muscles relax, you enter a sleepy state, and cannot perform well.

Therefore, it is necessary to train oneself to create a state that maintains the balance of sympathetic and parasympathetic nervous systems. The result of this balance will be a body that is in a fairly energetic state and a mind that is in a good, stable state such as heijoshin or mushin. When the hormones mentioned above are secreted in a well-balanced manner, the goal disappears and one's best performance is achieved. This may sound like a lofty explanation, but anxiety and stress are mere idle thoughts. When you look into what they really are, you find they are delusions. They don't exist in reality.

3

Methods of Relieving Anxiety

To deal with the pressure of a performance, many people in Japan say to imagine that everyone in the audience is a pumpkin. Others say, "Practice doing it many times, over and over, and you will get used to it," or "Write the character for 'person' on your palm (representing the people in the audience) and symbolically eat them." The idea is to put yourself in a stronger, predatory position to the audience—your prey. These methods may be effective for some people. However, for the general public these methods may not sound very realistic or scientific. Therefore, I would like to introduce a method with a more scientific basis.

(A) Food
Getting the Happiness Hormone (Serotonin) from What We Eat

The neurotransmitter serotonin is produced in the brainstem, much like dopamine. It is released when we eat well and do certain rhythmic exercises such as walking. It controls noradrenaline and dopamine, stabilizes the mind, and plays a role in removing anxiety and stress. For this reason, it is also called the "happiness hormone." This is the hormone that suppresses stress and anxiety.

Serotonin is not produced in the body directly. First, tryptophan is taken into the body from food such as soy, dairy, and grain. With the help of vitamin B6, tryptophan changes into serotonin in the brain when we are exposed to sunlight during the day. Then, serotonin changes into melatonin which promotes sleep at night.

In other words, the most efficient thing is to always have breakfast, and then if you spend about 15 minutes walking in the morning sun, happiness hormones will accumulate and last throughout the day. Sometimes I think when elderly people complain about something loudly at a reception desk and then become quiet when they are at home, it is because they are lacking such happiness hormones.

(B) Autogenic Training (AT)

In a broad sense, autogenic training is included in psychotherapy. That is because it has both a psychological and physiological effect. Autogenic training was founded in 1932 by Dr. Schultz in Germany. It is a psycho-physiological method of self-treatment that helps return balance through the function of the autonomic nervous system. It is also very useful for mental and physical stability. It is a cure. In sports, this method can relieve you of excessive tension and give you confidence. Your perception changes and your sports performance improves. This method was used in Japan during the 1964 Olympics on the athletes who had problems with tension and stress.

Autogenic training is a practice that includes repeating a specific determined phrase in your mind, at your own pace. Currently, autogenic training is used in mental practices, astronaut training, treating problems of the mind and body, and so forth. In other words, it helps maintain stability and relaxes the body.

The results of autogenic training are due to the regulatory effects of the **autonomic nervous system**. Autogenic training activates the **parasympathetic system** and causes it to **dominate the sympathetic nervous system**. This promotes mental calmness by causing the blood flow to increase and the muscles to relax. These effects further enhance the mind-body interaction and stabilize thoughts and emotions.

The essential mental state in traditional martial arts

is **kakusei-mushin.** After researching this state for five years, I reached a conclusion. The key is to maintain a state where the mind is not captured or fixed anywhere, and the body is able to respond immediately. One of the ways to create this state where your mind is not trapped anywhere, is through autogenic training. In addition, Zen meditation is also a good method, but it takes time and requires a good teacher. On the other hand, learning autogenic training only takes a short time, about five minutes per set, three sets per day. It is also simple to learn and doesn't require an instructor. I will explain it here.

First, consider your surroundings. The practice area should be somewhere as quiet as possible. You should also feel comfortable. Make sure you don't feel too hungry or have to use the toilet before beginning. Next, find a relaxing posture. This can be lying on your back or sitting in a chair, however you feel comfortable. Then, close your eyes gently and take a few deep breaths. From here, I will explain the official practice.

First, to reset your feelings, repeat the following phrase in your mind: "I feel calm, I feel calm, I feel calm." Next, imagine a heavy feeling in your arms and legs and repeat the following phrases: "My right arm feels heavy, My right arm feels heavy, My right arm feels heavy." Then, "My left arm feels heavy, My left arm feels heavy, My left arm feels heavy." Next, "My right leg feels heavy, My right leg feels heavy, My right leg feels heavy." Then, "My left leg feels heavy, My left leg feels heavy, My left leg feels heavy."

Continue imagining that heavy feeling in your body and repeat the first phrase again: "I feel calm, I feel calm, I feel calm." Next, imagine a warm feeling as though you are soaking your hands and feet in warm water. Repeat the following phrases: "My right arm is warm, My right arm is warm, My right arm is warm. My left arm is warm, My left arm is warm, My left arm is warm." Then, "My right leg is warm, My right leg is warm, My right leg is warm. My left leg is warm, My left leg is warm, My left leg is warm."

Finally, clear your mind with the following set of exercises. First, open and close your hands many times quickly. Next, straighten and bend your arms (as if punching) several times quickly. Then, extend your arms and gently stretch your back. Return your arms to their normal position and open your eyes. From the time you close your eyes until you open them again should take about 90 seconds. There is no additional effect for doing it longer. Repeat this three times. You can complete three sets within five minutes.

Here are some important notes on the practice. In autogenic training, it's important to feel the condition of your body. You aren't trying to *make* your arms and legs become heavy or warm. You don't say, "Become heavy, become heavy." The key is to *feel* the heaviness and warmth that is there. It's important to feel the condition passively, rather than try to force it to happen.

Finally, it's important to do the clearing and wake-up procedure at the end. The purpose of this is to awaken the mind and body. If you do not do this, your muscles may remain too relaxed and interfere with your other activities that day.

I explained the very basics above, but there are many other official methods of doing it. However, just doing the 'heavy' and 'warm' version can achieve the desired effect. The other important thing is to feel comfortable when you are finished.

I have been doing this 'heavy-warm' version of autogenic training every day for the past five years. As a result, no matter what form stress comes in, if I just accept that, "Ok, stress came," I automatically feel better now. Unconsciously, the autonomic nerves (sympathetic and parasympathetic) become well balanced, relieving me from anxiety and stress. This frees my mind from annoyance and my mental state remains calm. This allows me to maintain heijoshin.

(C) Mindfulness

The study of *mindfulness* began to attract the attention of clinical psychologists in the mid-1980s and the number of papers began to increase rapidly from the early 2000s. The goal is to naturally acquire an open state of mind where your attention is not taken in or captured by anything.

In Japan, in the mid-1600s, a high priest of the Rinzai sect named Takuan Soho taught the Zen lesson of *kenzen-ichinyo* to Yagyu Tajima-no-kami Munenori. The teaching comes from the work *Fudochishin-myoroku*. The expression *kenzen-ichinyo* means that the lessons in sword fighting and the lessons in Zen are ultimately the same. The first thing that is written in this work is, "Being distracted by polluted thoughts leads you astray." This means that when your mind gets stuck on something, you will be cut down.

Mindfulness was derived from a meditation called *Vipassana* from the Theravada Buddhist tradition which began over 2500 years ago. Consequently, the aim of mindfulness and the quiet mind that is pursued in Zen, are exactly the same.

Another way of looking at mindfulness is that it is a way of observing oneself or paying attention to the present moment. **Mindfulness is a skill that allows one to distinguish between delusion and reality.**

Ordinary people tend to put these delusions or "wild ideas" in their head together with reality. Then, they have trouble distinguishing between the two and their anxiety over an imagined idea grows bigger and bigger. This results in the accumulation of unnecessary stress. As I mentioned before, noradrenaline is secreted and causes one's stress level to stay high. However, one can get out of this situation through mindfulness, even though this was not the original purpose of mindfulness practice.

Whether through mindfulness or autogenic training, it becomes possible to activate the parasympathetic nervous system and secrete serotonin, bringing you into a balanced state. In addition, you can suppress the secretion of noradrenaline (which causes stress), through these practices. The result of all this is that you will be released from stress and anxiety.

Next, I will introduce you to the specific mindfulness method taught by Dr. Hiroaki Kumano, Professor of Medicine at Waseda University.

1) How to Look at Yourself Objectively

This is effective during times when you repeatedly think about something negative in the past, or when you repeatedly think about what you should do if such a negative situation arises.

If you cannot distinguish between your imaginative fears and reality, your anxiety will grow and you will have more stress. In such a case, saying to yourself "It's just a thought" after having a stressful thought such as "What should I do?" or "What's going on, What's going on?" will reduce the feeling of anxiety quickly. This is called *Cognitive Defusion.* **It's the process of allowing problematic thoughts to come and go without getting caught up in them.** You will begin to see yourself objectively and realize, "It was because of my delusional, imaginative fear that I was seeing things unclearly.

2) Perceive Reality Through Breathing

This breathing method is effective when you are

mentally tired, your attention is distracted, or you can't control your emotions. Pay attention to your current situation as you breathe. For example, if you sit down, you can pay attention to breathing through your nose, the expanding and contracting of your abdomen as you breathe, feeling hungry, and so forth. If you are walking, you can focus on breathing in through the nose for a three count, and breathing out for a three count. If you have distracting thoughts, you can chant the word *zatsunen* (distracting thoughts), in your head to make the distracting thoughts dissolve themselves. Another method is to simply count your breaths repeatedly.

3) Listen to the Sounds Around You

This is effective during times when you are easily distracted, when you can't seem to change how you feel, or when you don't have good attentiveness.

Stage One:
Count how many sounds you can hear around you. Choose one of them and focus on that sound for one minute. After one minute, choose a different sound and focus on that for one minute. Repeat this process for five to six minutes.

Stage Two:
Reduce the amount of time you spent focusing on the sounds in stage one. Choose one sound and move to the next in 15-20 seconds. Repeat this process for five to six

minutes.

Stage Three:
Listen to all the sounds at the same time. At first, it will be good if you can do this for two to three minutes. Finally, expand the space around you in your mind and create an image of the sounds coming towards you from all the various directions.

4) The Walking Method

This is effective in cases when you are concerned about the people around you watching, when you want to solve a problem, or when you want to look at a problem from a new perspective. In a place where you are surrounded by nature, such as in a park or in the woods, walk step by step taking in all of your surroundings. You are free to walk in any style and at any pace. Walk in your favorite place at your favorite speed. In your mind as you walk, consciously choose to take each step. As mentioned above, practicing **Professor Kumano's mindfulness method is an effective way to free yourself from stress and anxiety.**

It is extremely important to remember the feelings in your mind and body immediately after doing either autogenic training or practicing mindfulness. Once you remember that feeling, the mind and body start becoming conditioned to be in that state. The parasympathetic nervous system becomes activated like a conditioned reflex by the repeated practice of the autogenic and mindfulness training. Through my own experience, I can confirm that the hormones that cause anxiety and stress become suppressed.

(D) The Method of Kakusei-Mushin

What is kakusei-mushin?

When I was a graduate research student at the University of Tsukuba, I researched the conditions under which the mental and physical aspects of mushin could be effectively achieved. These conditions included *susokukan* (a meditation method of counting breathes), and maintaining focus on one's *tanden* (the place on the body just below the navel). Let's consider the terms mushin, heijoshin, and fudoshin.

First of all, I noticed that there were two sides, a mental side and a physical side, of mushin, heijoshin, and fudoshin. Professor Sakairi from the University of Tsukuba mentions that both the "activation of the brain" and the "activation of the body" are set to "off" in mushin. In the state of mushin, people don't speak or think. However, the activation of the brain is set to "off" and the "activation of the body" is set to "on" in the state called *kakusei-mushin*, which I will define later in this book. He also mentions that the body's activation is like being on automatic pilot, while the brain's activation is like manual driving. I think these points are easy for anybody to understand. This is how the mental aspect is created, which is the secret of martial arts. It is where the mind, technique, and body all come together as one.

The descriptions below are the results of my analysis, but this book only describes the conclusions. If you are interested in more information, please refer to the book Kakusei-Mushin, which explains my research as a graduate student at the University of Tsukuba.

(1) About Mushin:
(a) What is the mental side of mushin?
Mushin is a state in which a person understands everything around them, but is not trapped by anything. He/she is capable of noticing even a pin drop. It is how the previously described books, such as Fudochishin-myoroku, The Book of Five Rings, and the scrolls from various traditional martial arts schools, describe it. The head of each school tends to teach the same thing, but puts it into different words. When the mind lets go of the things that trap it, one enters into a state called mushin, which allows a person to ideally react to threats. This is the origin of mushin and it is how I understand mushin.

If you hear a sound when your mind is in this state, you recognize the sound without thinking of where it comes from or what causes it. If you see a forest, you will recognize the many trees and many colors without thinking about the details. Similarly, it is important to *not* pay attention to each move of your opponent's body when their body is moving fast in the midst of a battle. From here, when your own body then moves automatically, without thought, I define that state as kakusei-mushin. I will elaborate more on this in the next chapter.

(b) What is the physical side of mushin?

Ekiken Kaibara (1630-1714) says in his book, Yojokun, volume 2, p.48 that, "The tanden (the area just below one's navel) is filled with energy. Whoever performs a technique involving a lot of energy should always straighten the waist to focus on the tanden. Maintain calm breathing, breathe lightly from the chest many times when doing something, and focus energy on the tanden, not the chest. Warriors training for battle should pay attention to this. Especially anyone who does actual fighting. Bushi for example, should know how to do this."

So how does one gather energy in the tanden? The method I use is to stand in a natural posture and lower my center. Then, I shift my weight from side to side. This allows me to feel the tension in my lower abdomen as I shift my body weight from leg to leg. While doing this, the bottom of my feet grip the ground. I put slightly more weight towards my toes. I bend my knees a little and keep my face and upper body straight. I experience the energy in the tanden through different bodily sensations.

Another good thing about the tanden is that it's in

the center of the body. Thus, a person focusing on their tanden can stabilize their body, making it difficult to fall. This is a state in which the body does not have unnecessary tension or stress, and one can move freely in reaction to an opponent's moves, similar to when water flows according to the shape of the ground.

It is the physical version of the state that Takuan Soho teaches in his book Fudochishin-myoroku. In the book, he gives several examples.

(2) About Heijoshin

Here is what the book says using an example situation of being surrounded by 100 enemies. "There are two ways to get out of this predicament. The first way is to find a timid person, the second is to find the leader." You can survive by defeating either one. There is a similar example from Musashi Miyamoto, who defeated the leader of a crowd in the Yoshioka School when he was a child. Musashi's act is from a "level mind" or "calm mind." Similar to mushin, it is easy to understand that heijoshin has a spiritual and physical side to it.

(a) What is the mental side of heijoshin?

I define it as "the mind that is made from the accumulation of day to day training." We should consider maintaining mental heijoshin as a goal. Then, as I mentioned before, we can assess the situation of the enemy from a broad perspective, find the truth, and use various strategies. By maintaining heijoshin, we keep our focus and accomplish our goal. Then based on the opponent's moves, we accomplish the task from a state of mushin and leave.

Actively analyzing information about the enemy's condition is important in life and death situations. Without the mental side of heijoshin, it would be nearly impossible to estimate the situation accurately.

(b) What is the physical side of heijoshin?

I define it as "the movements the body has learned from hard daily training." In other words, it is a state in which we can react according to the circumstances without thinking, just like a conditioned reflex when there is a sudden attack. In such a spiritual/mental state, the body moves freely. Paying attention to one's body movements can stop the flow. Therefore, we should create the mental and physical states without tension in our bodies. This leads to kakusei-mushin.

In volume three of Sun Tzu's book the Art of War, a character named Boukou, says,"You can win all battles if you know both yourself and your enemy. You have a fifty percent chance of winning if you know yourself but not your enemy. You are always in danger if you know neither yourself nor your enemy."

This means that you can win if you understand the balance of the power between you and your enemy and can find a way to use it to your advantage. Also, it indicates that finding weak points in the enemy through calm observation is key.

(3) About Fudoshin

In general, the term "fudoshin" refers to a mind that does not move, such as a big rock. However, I believe that I can divide it into a mental side and a physical side, such as previously described with mushin and heijoshin.

(a) What is the mental side of fudoshin?

I define it as "the mind which cannot be disrupted" or "the mind which does not move." It is a state of mind in which a person does not give up, no matter who his opponent is, if he believes his act is right.

You are not in fudoshin if your mind gets upset because of what someone says or does.

(b) What is the physical side of fudoshin?

I define it as a state of the body in which one can immediately adapt to corresponding changes in the conditions. It is not the state of "not moving at all no matter what happens," like a big rock. It is a stable state in which you can immediately react to the circumstances.

In martial arts, lowering and stabilizing the body while maintaining tension in the tanden makes you move more effectively. This allows you to avoid the opponent's attacks. This is the physical side of fudoshin.

(E) Developing Heijoshin, Mushin, and Fudoshin

This is what I have been searching for, for over fifty years. The result is now backed by a comprehensive analysis in human science. This has revealed the ultimate secrets of mushin, heijoshin, and fudoshin, over which many predecessors have fought to develop through blood and sweat.

(1) Developing the Physical and Mental States of Heijoshin and Fudoshin

I always think that it is important to be ready to adapt automatically when an enemy is attacking in a very unexpected moment, such as in the middle of the night. Therefore, **we must include training that exceeds our limitations of physical strength and vitality into our regular training.** Doing so allows for more confidence and improvements in mental alertness. This is important for developing heijoshin and fudoshin.

In fact, all the world's special forces use this exact method. However, no matter how trained you are, there are differences in a real battle. In my opinion, a trained mind in heijoshin should be able to observe situations while maintaining a normal feeling. But in an actual fight, it may be necessary to use a higher skill, such as mushin.

(2) Functions of the Body

First, we will take a closer look at our general brain functions (such as collecting and analyzing information,

28

making decisions for the best action, muscle movement commands for different parts of the body, correct body movement, etc.)

Our body has five basic senses: sight, sound, taste, smell, and touch. These senses can be divided into three categories: **special sensation** (sight, sound, taste, smell, balance), **somatic sensation** (cutaneous sensation: touch and pain, temperature/proprioception: pressure, position, muscle and motion sensation) and **visceral sensation** (hungry or full, urinary or fecal sensation, visceral pain). I'll discuss how to sense the enemy based on the teachings of "know thy enemy, know thyself, and you shall never lose in a hundred battles."

First, any information obtained from the eyes, ears, tongue, nose, or skin is converted into electrical signals in various areas by special sensation (sight, sound, taste, smell, balance) and somatic sensation (cutaneous sensation, touch, pain, temperature) receptors. Those signals are then transferred to other areas of the brain (frontal lobe, parietal lobe, occipital lobe and temporal lobe). We gather information about the enemy through the use of these senses.

Second, I'll discuss how to know oneself. Your own **somatic sensation** (proprioception, pressure, position, muscle or motion sensation) and **visceral sensation** (hungry or full, urinary or fecal sensation, visceral pain) are converted into an electrical signals and transferred to the cerebrum, cerebellum and brainstem. This allows you to understand your own condition.

Third, the brain forms an action plan and conveys orders. The brain formulates a plan in the prefrontal cortex based on logic, motion control, and future predictions. That information is stored and gets sent to other parts of the brain. Those signals are then transmitted to the premotor cortex to plan details about various procedures and to give directions to the motor cortex. The motor cortex controls voluntary movements in the body by influencing nerve cells which correspond to different parts of the body.

The cerebellum is there to assure that the operation is going as planned and to make corrections as necessary. The cerebellum may correct or fine-tune necessary distances, power, or speed, by obtaining information from previously described sensations. In other words, the cerebellum is adjusting for any gaps in the operational plan ordered by the cerebrum.

During the above operation, various things will happen. In order to activate physical exercise, both adrenaline and noradrenaline are released into the blood stream to activate the sympathetic nerves, activate the muscle movement, increase the heart rate by increasing glucose levels to release energy from fat, increase myocardial contractibility to increase the blood supply, and dilate blood vessels to increase oxygen supply through respiration. It also minimizes the amount of bleeding caused by injuries by contracting the blood vessels of skin and mucous membranes.

Moreover, use of digestive organs is reduced in order to provide maximum energy for fighting. In order to allow you to continue fighting, adrenaline blocks pain signals. There have even been cases in war where people were completely unaware that they had lost their arm or leg. The above is the physical functioning of the body from a physiological view.

(3) Mental and Physical Aspects of Mushin

From the expression, "Know thy enemy, know thyself, and you shall never lose in a hundred battles," let's first consider the "knowing your enemy" part. A crucial part of knowing your enemy is learning to let go of anything that distracts you or pulls you in a particular direction. Mushin can only be achieved if you can let go of the things that capture/distract you. This is the foundation of mushin.

It is a formidable challenge to completely understand the entire surrounding situation without giving off any feelings. Still, if you can manage to control your feelings, it is a step closer to achieving the state of mushin.

I don't want you to have the wrong idea here. Mushin is not being "relaxed." Again, the state of mushin is by no means just a matter of being relaxed.

How to Develop Mushin:

The first way to develop the mental aspect of

mushin is through the susokukan (counting breaths) meditation. One of the basic training methods in Zen is to first sit in either a position called kekka-fuza (lotus position) or hanka-fuza (half-lotus position). From this position, one concentrates on doing the susokukan meditation (focusing on breathing in and out while counting from 1 to 100). Continue doing this repeatedly until you reach a state of concentration called *susoku-sanmai* (counting-breaths-samadhi) a state of intense meditative concentration.

Next, you will enter a stage called *zenjo-zanmai,* or *dhyana-samadhi.* This is different from *munen-muso*, (a state where your mind is empty of all thought, like a trance). For example, if there is a sound while you are in samadhi, you are aware of it, but don't develop worldly thoughts about it such as "What kind of sound is it?" Or, "Where did it come from?" In samadhi, you're aware of the sound but you don't think about it. It doesn't pull your attention away.

In a different state called munen-muso, you don't hear anything around you. I'm getting off topic, but the mind and body mechanism during meditation is as follows.

When Zen and yoga masters do zazen or other meditations, electroencephalograms show augmentation of alpha waves in the frontal part of the brain, as well as rhythmical theta waves. A scientific study has shown that yoga masters and Zen masters have different reactions to external stimulation during meditation. Yoga masters showed no signs of alpha wave blocking due to external stimulation, while Zen masters did show signs of blocking. This implies that the Zen masters heard the sound (resulting in disrupted alpha waves), while the yoga masters did not (no disruption). This result has yet to be confirmed by subsequent studies.

Translator's note: Alpha waves are associated with an awake, relaxed state with one's eyes closed. Disruption or blocking of these waves is evidence of arousal (such as becoming aware of a sound). Manaka Unsui has elaborated on this study in class, saying that Zen meditation is better suited for martial artists than yoga meditation because Zen masters maintained an awareness of their surroundings during meditation (recognized sounds), while yoga masters did not (no alpha wave blocking).

Another characteristic brain wave pattern during meditation is high amplitude theta waves in the frontal midline of the brain. Theta waves are seen not only when one is relaxed, but also when one is working on tasks involving high concentration.

The tanden breathing method during zazen was confirmed to increase blood flow to the prefrontal cortex area. A big increase in hemoglobin was also seen. This helps maintain the meditative state by decreasing theta waves and increasing alpha waves, which in turn makes a person feel better. Also, an additional increase of serotonin balances the mind. Pain sensations during zazen involve cortical areas of the brain. Brain structure can change (cortical areas can thicken) in those who practice meditation for many years.

Developing the Physical Aspect of Mushin:

The second way to develop the physical aspect of mushin is to keep tension in one's tanden (the area just below the navel). First, we need to create a state of *tanden tension*. With your back straight, and head facing forward, relax your shoulders. Start to feel your tanden. From this position, shift your weight left and right and begin to feel the tension in your tanden. Both feet must be grounded on the floor and your weight should be slightly forward, towards your toes. Flex your knees a little and maintain a straight position with your head and torso.

This tanden tension is the physical sensation that I personally experience when concentrating my mind on the tanden. Maintaining this state completes the physical state of mushin. Practicing the susokukan meditation described earlier while maintaining this state with tension on the tanden will take you into both the physical and mental realms of mushin.

Since ancient times, Japan has been using expressions such as "put strength in your abdomen" and "have guts." These expressions are frequently used to instruct martial artists and other students in various fields.

Also, as mentioned earlier, the *Yojokun* (The Book of Life-Nourishing Principles) written by Ekiken Kaibara, says, "The energy of life gathers in the area three *sun* (a unit of measurement roughly equal to an inch) down the navel. In order to foster spiritual strength, one must have the correct posture and breathe deeply. One must put tension on the abdomen without attracting any feeling to the mind. This way, power in body can be nourished without any distraction. When samurai train in martial arts, they must always remember this mental attitude, even when battling with enemies. Samurai and those who use weapons should understand this technique."

Additionally, Musashi Miyamoto has said, "Tighten your abdomen so that the lower back does not round. Like tightening a wedge, bring your abdomen close to the sheath of the sword."

I believe this has two meanings in regard to using the sheath of the short sword. The first meaning refers to a method which easily focuses on the tanden by putting pressure on the lower abdomen. The second meaning refers to a method of drawing a sword with the left hand only. This can be done by wearing a tight *obi,* instead of using your left thumb to break the sheath's frictional pressure holding the sword in place.

From here, your mind will no longer be attached to things. But what kind of physical change can be observed after experiencing the new state of kakusei-mushin and ultimately mushin?

At first, your mind becomes calm by activating the prefrontal cortex. Doing this supplies serotonin, which balances the mind by suppressing the use of noradrenaline and dopamine. Not enough serotonin may cause one to become violent or exhibit depression. Proper serotonin levels help balance the mind and suppress the release of noradrenaline and dopamine. Additionally, serotonin in the blood has other functions such as hemostasis and vasoconstriction, which is one the causes of migraines.

The causes of inadequate serotonin levels come from excessive use of computers, video games, lack of exercise, and reversed day/night sleeping rhythms. Therefore, if you maintain a normal life and do some exercise, as well as get a little sun every day, serotonin levels will naturally return to normal.

(F) Maintaining Kakusei-Mushin and Heijoshin

*The author has done kesa-giri (a diagonal cut downward) through the bamboo and is preparing to do a second cut upwards called kiri-age.

I've mentioned kakusei-mushin, heijoshin, and fudoshin many times, but here I would like to take a look at why it is so difficult to maintain these states. Humans hold many worldly thoughts. These worldly thoughts make us think about unnecessary matters and as a result, we experience a lack of concentration.

You can see the problem through the teachings of Dr. Sakairi, who is a psychology professor at the University of Tsukuba. He explains, "Humans have two minds. One is in the brain, and the other is in the body." He believes that when the state or continuity of mushin is broken, one's movements become awkward. This is caused by the *mind of brain* and the *mind of body* interacting with each other.

In my opinion, heijoshin can be nurtured through everyday training. You should continue training until you are able to properly respond to unexpected attacks during sleep. As a result, you can easily analyze any situation and be able to have the correct judgement about your enemy's movements. Then, you can take correct measures based on the situation. At that point, the mind and body can enter the state of kakusei-mushin. Fudoshin is a state which you may experience with proper training if you remain committed and have strong confidence.

Mencius describes fudoshin as follows: "My mind became stable after the age of forty. Spirit can be affected by will, which is the key element of the mind. It is the spirit which controls the human body. If one's will is strong enough, spirit will follow. Will and spirit are closely related to each other."

Confucius described it when he said, "If I have just cause, I shall take action even if there are thousands of enemies."

Furthermore, a way to develop fudoshin during daily training is to maintain kakusei-mushin or heijoshin, and not change from that state. Self-meditation, in which you imagine an ideal movement, is another possible method of training. Similar to your body, your brain will remember the same state or awareness level with repeated practice.

It is difficult to prevent having idle thoughts. Therefore, it is important to be aware of when you begin having such thoughts. Although autogenic training is an effective way to train this skill, no one has yet verified how autogenic training and mindfulness are reflected in martial arts. Hence, this matter should be further explored in the future.

(G) The Mindset During Normal Training

*The author cuts through bamboo with a long sword and a short sword at the same instant.

I will repeat myself once again here. Always self-check your mental state of kakusei-mushin at the beginning of training and during training. However, it is an extremely high hurdle for beginners to maintain this state while acquiring new skills. Every attempt is an important chance to improve. As I said previously, it is difficult to prevent having idle thoughts. Thus, it is important to become aware of them when they begin occurring.

Moreover, correctly learning heijoshin and kakusei-mushin and not changing from such a state is a way to develop what is called fudoshin during daily training. Training should also include awareness of one's surroundings and letting go of any worldly thoughts. In addition, I believe autogenic training is an effective method for refreshing a tired body and mind. Ultimately, it is best not to think about it directly, but rather maintain this state without thinking of it as kakusei-mushin.

Kakusei-mushin is the ideal mental state for top athletes to enter, in order to give their best performance.

4

Conclusion

So far, I have described autogenic training, mindfulness, and kakusei-mushin as methods of relieving stress and anxiety. But whichever method one chooses, the key is to remember the feeling in one's body after the training is finished. In addition, it is good to measure your heart-rate at the end of the training.

Please refer to the following figures:

175 Beats Per Minute:
When your heart-rate goes over 175 beats per minute, complex motor skills become nearly impossible. Your body may involuntarily urinate and/or defecate. However, simple motor skills such as running can reach peak levels.

115-145 Beats Per Minute:

When your heart-rate is at this level, complex motor skills, cognitive response skills, and visual recognition skills are at their best.

60-80 Beats Per Minute:

When your heart-rate is at this level, your motor skills decline. This is the normal rate when you are at rest.

Everyone is a little different but try to find a method that works for you. You should try to maintain a heart-rate of approximately 130 beats per minute. In various sports, the longer the wait time between performances, the more difficult it will be to maintain mushin or heijoshin.

When you see other people's performances you will be comparing them to your own. If you failed or did poorly on your last performance, you will also be dragging that along with you. These kinds of things make it difficult to switch one's mindset. However, I believe that in such cases, autogenic training, mindfulness, and kakusei-mushin, are all effective. The body (one's muscles) have already been completely trained to do the performance. So, if you can keep your mind calm, you should be able to do the performance at your best.

Again, this book is not aimed just at top athletes. These methods are my recommendations for the general public to benefit from mushin and heijoshin.

Whether you are about to give a speech or do a performance in front of many people, this kind of change in your environment can cause stress levels to rise. As I have explained in this book, it's not a matter of weak people training to strengthen their mind. Instead, it is about bringing balance to the autonomic nervous system to maintain a calm state.

Putting these methods into practice doesn't require any money or medicine. Obviously, there are no harmful side-effects. All you need is the *will* to put one of these methods into practice. Once you generate the will, you can set specific goals. Once you have specific goals, you will have the motivation to move forward and make them happen. Many psychosomatic doctors from around the world have also been taking advantage of these methods to treat patients. **Everyone, please find a way which suits you and try it.**

*Translator's note: Psychosomatic medicine is a branch of psychiatry that deals with the relation between mental and physical illnesses.

Finally, I would like to thank Dr. Rei Amemiya, Professor of Psychology at the University of Tsukuba, for his guidance on this book. I would also like to give a big thanks to Mr. Hiroaki Kato (a colleague from the National Defense Academy of Japan), and Kazuhiro Iida (yondan in the Jinenkan), who were in charge of editing the Japanese version of this book. I would also like to thank Robert Gray (yondan in the Jinenkan) for translating this book into English. The many references and quotation sources I used when writing this book have been placed in the bibliography at the end. Everyone, thank you very much.

5

Bibliography

Old Document: The Seven Military Classics. Sen Suharaya Mohei. Edo Nihonbashi. November, 1795.

Old Document: Great Learning, The Constant Mean, Mencius, Analects. Tomigi, Fushimiya Emon. Shorin 1828. Republished by Inuko Kishun

Old Document: Book of Documents. I Ching. Book of Poetry. Book of Rites. Spring and Autumn Annals. Sasuke, Kawachiya. Osaka Shorin.

Old Document: Fudochishin-myoroku. Takuan, Soho. Higashi-Hieizan. Edo Shitaya Onari Do Seiundo. English version.

Self-Control of the Mind and Body in Sports, "Meditation and Frontal Lobe Functions," Sakairi Yosuke, Physical Education Science 58 (2), 2008

Influence of Muscle Tone and Behavioral Reactions from Postures in Kendo. Human Science Vol. 23 No. 1. Akihiro Ito, Kana Unbi, Takeshi Shimizu, Motoshima Namiko. Sakairi, Yosuke. Human Science Council, May 26, 2014.

Standard Autonomic Training Textbook, Second Edition, Japan Autonomic Training Society Education Committee, September 2012.

Kakusei-Mushin, Fumio Manaka, Jinenkan, 2017.

Introductory Lecture on Mindfulness, Akira Osamu, Kongo Publishing Co., Ltd.

An Introduction to Mindfulness, Japan Broadcasting Association / NHK Publishing.

Current Health Care Science, Waseda University Research Center for Human Science, Satoshi Ishii, Corona Co., January 11, 2008.

Fudochishin-myoroku, Takuan Soho, Translator: Satoshi Ikeda. Tokuma Shoten, 1972.

An Introduction to Zen, Horashiki Haga, Million books, November, 1963.

Zen, Tainen Matsuo, Kainan Shobo, August 26, 1973.

The Book of Five Rings, Miyamoto Musashi, Translation by Tadashi Kamiko, Tokuma Shoten, 1973.

Yojokun (The Book of Life-Nourishing Principles), Ekiken Kaibara, Translation by Tomonobu Ito, Kodansha Bunko, December 1, 1991.

Yojokun Contemporary Text, Ekiken Kaibara, Translation by Masayuki Morishita, Hara Shobo, June 1, 2002.

Understanding the Brain, Makoto Iwata, Natsume Inc., September 10, 2014.

Mencius, Vol. 1 and 2, Kobayashi Katsuhito, Iwanami Bunko, February, 1968.

On Combat, Dave Grossman, Loren W. Christensen, Translated by Kazumi Yasuhara, Futami Shobo, March 25, 2008.

On Killing, Dave Grossman, Translated by Kazumi Yasuhara, Chikuma Shobo, June 20, 2010.

An Electroencephalographic Study on Zen Meditation (ZAZEN), Akira Kasamatsu M.D. and Tomio Hirai M.D. Article first published online March 17, 2008.

Activation of the anterior prefrontal cortex and Serotonergic system is associated with improvements in mood and EEG changes induced by Zen meditation practice in novices. Xinjun Yu, Masaki Fumoto, Yasushi Nakatani, Tamami Sekiyama, Hiromi Kikuchi, Yoshinari Seki, Ikuko Sato Suzuki, Hideho Arita, October 2010.

Cortical thickness and pain sensitivity in Zen meditators, Joshua A. Grant, Jeromei Courtemanche, Emma G. Duerden, Gary H. Duncan, Pierre Rainville, Emotion, Vol. 10 (1), February 2010, p. 43-53.

www.ingramcontent.com/pod-product-compliance
Lightning Source LLC
Chambersburg PA
CBHW032036090426
42741CB00006B/843